The richness I achieve comes from Nature, the source of my inspiration. CLAUDE MONET

It's morning again, little hope, and the world's
drying off with fresh-laundered sunshine.
Life's face is never the same though we may
look at it for all eternity

MARY OLIVER

Keep close to Nature's heart...and break
clear away, once in a while, and climb a
mountain or spend a week in the woods.
Wash your spirit clean. **JOHN MUIR**

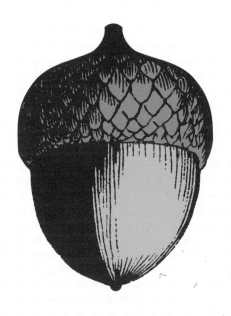

O world, I cannot
hold thee close enough!

EDNA ST. VINCENT MILLAY

Look deep into nature, and then you will understand everything better. ALBERT EINSTEIN

One must ask children and birds
how cherries and strawberries taste.

JOHANN WOLFGANG VON GOETHE

You can never
have too much sky.
SANDRA CISNEROS